'*Refreshing in its simplicity. This is no ordinary instruction to pray [but] a book that can be enjoyed by individuals of all religious persuasion, including those who feel they have none. Long's simple message pierced my cynical armour.*'

NOVA HOLISTIC JOURNAL

'*Clear, precise and very direct. A book for those who are honest and courageous enough to look at the truth, just as it is. Highly recommended.*'

GOLDEN AGE

IT LOOKS LIKE CIVILISATION IS AT A CRITICAL POINT. APPARENTLY WE can live with wars, disease, poverty, conflict, even appalling acts of terrorism. But what of the global threat – worldwide calamity, the collapse of civilisation, total destruction? How can we live with that? Or live through it? How did we ever get ourselves into this? Have we got a hope?

Barry Long's 'A Prayer for Life' is a plea for us to wake up to the appalling truth of our situation, and to the calamitous human condition that unknowingly perpetuates suffering and misery while devoutly wishing and hoping for change.

This book is a radical and challenging perspective on human history. We are shown our complacency and ignorance of our God-given life. What have we been doing wrong, that we can change?

BARRY LONG IS A SPIRITUAL MASTER RECOGNISED WORLDWIDE. HE was born in 1926 in Australia and lives in northern New South Wales. His spiritual realisation began in the early 1960s and was provoked by self-enquiry independent of any religious tradition. He began teaching in London in the late 1960s. By the 1990s he was travelling the world speaking of love, life and truth. He is now acknowledged as one of the leading spiritual masters of our times. Barry Long's unique hallmark is his down-to-earth, direct communication immediately accessible to anyone. His work has been published in ten languages.

Also by Barry Long

Only Fear Dies
Meditation A Foundation Course
Stillness Is The Way
The Way In – A book of self-discovery
The Origins of Man and the Universe
Knowing Yourself
Wisdom and Where to Find It
To Woman In Love
To Man In Truth
Making Love: Sexual Love the Divine Way
Raising Children in Love, Justice and Truth

Audio Books
Start Meditating Now
A Journey in Consciousness
Seeing Through Death
Making Love
How To Live Joyously

BARRY LONG

A PRAYER FOR

Life

**The Cause and Cure of
Terrorism, War
and Human Suffering**

BARRY LONG BOOKS

First published 2002

BARRY LONG BOOKS
BCM Box 876, London WC1N 3XX, UK
Box 5277, Gold Coast MC, Queensland 4217, Australia
6230 Wilshire Blvd - Suite 251, Los Angeles, CA 90048, USA
www.barrylong.org   info@barrylong.org

This book is the revised and extended text of an audio cassette
first recorded and released by The Barry Long Foundation in 1984
with the title 'The End of the World'.

Cataloguing-In-Publication Data:
A catalogue record for this book is available from The British Library.
Library of Congress Catalog Card Number: 2002090001

ISBN 1 899324 17 8

Back cover photo: Rita Newman
Printed in Singapore

CONTENTS

FOREWORD

*B*arry Long is a spiritual master – a man acknowledged as having overcome fear and suffering in himself, who can explain our human condition in ways that help us free ourselves. He is a teacher who speaks and writes about the underlying causes of unhappiness, greed, frustration, ambition, hatred – to remind us of love, or the one original cause, God. He queries the prevailing values of our world, society, family and civilisation, to alert us to a priceless value, well beyond worth or sentiment. He may pose a question, propose a solution, provoke, challenge or confirm our own perceptions but he will not persuade us to believe in anything that we do not find to be true. We must seek our own solutions, take responsibility for our own lives. And yet the spiritual master is provided in a hostile world as an exemplar for those whose inner call is to reject the false and inessential in favour of the truth.

When it comes to matters of life and death, almost everyone turns to God, some higher power, or the spirit. The danger passes: everyday life returns to godless normality.

A mortal threat to me and mine is bad enough. What of a global threat? How can we accept that the earth itself, or all of life as we know it, is sentenced to death? Even if we could accept it, would anything change?

Would we change? Millennial projections of Armageddon over a couple of thousand years came and went. In the 20th century we learned to live with the threat of nuclear holocaust. We easily forget or ignore how fragile we are. In the 1980s Barry Long predicted that paranational terror would soon shake our civilisation and that many as yet inconceivable horrors would be visited upon the earth. His prophecies and message were hard to hear – and few even listened. Now in the opening years of the new millennium we are faced with prophecies coming true. And many more people are listening.

In this book Barry Long offers anew his appraisal of the prospects for humanity. In the light of world events, he gives us his latest observations on the fate of civilisation. He pinpoints the cause and cure of conflict, war and suffering, not just on a global scale but in the daily lives of everyone – for who does not have a personal interest in survival?

In times of trouble we offer up our prayers, little knowing why or what effect they have. Barry Long's radical perspective challenges our preconceptions, and will devastate any complacency. Yet this book is truly a prayer for life – not laden with doom, but an uplifting vision of a much vaster life than we are normally permitted to know.

Clive Tempest

AUTHOR'S NOTE

*T*he horrific tragedy of the terrorist attack on the World Trade Centre towers in New York on 11 September 2001 has prompted me to issue as a separate book this revised and greatly expanded text of my prophetic audio tape 'The End of the World', first published in 1984. A revised version of the original text is also included in my book 'The Way In' published in 2000.

After 11 September I was moved to write more about the implications of the attack and the cause of terrorism. These new sections, 17 short chapters, are added here.

I strongly advise you to read from the beginning, even if you have come across some of the material before; and not skip to the new. Normal curiosity may encourage that, but without the understanding derived from reading the whole book, what I have to say becomes just another worldly topic for debate or discussion.

I trust that what is said here will make a difference in the lives of those who can hear, and through them in generations yet to come.

To me the tragic topicality of the subject matter makes it imperative for someone to start revealing cause beyond the usual blaming and accusations for the ills of the world. This in no way is to excuse individual actions that destroy life and lives indiscriminately. But it is to say that every event in existence is an effect of innumerable previous effects. And that it's time to get back to the cause – for people to understand the source, past and current, of the relentless mounting degeneration of the world that is marring, and in many cases destroying, the lives of people of all cultures.

Remember, the 'End of the World' tape was written in 1983 and the events predicted have taken many years to manifest as the extreme condition of the world today. Time is beyond the scope of prophets. Time is its own master.

Barry Long
November 2001

'I suspect that the swallows will still fly
and the children will still sing.'

Barry Long

THE FORCE OF PRAYER

THE UNSUSPECTED

*W*e human beings have been praying since time began. Whatever we've been praying for doesn't seem to have done much good. Is the world as good as it is, or as bad as it is, because of our prayers? Either way is not much of a recommendation for prayer, is it?

If our prayers ended the last global war 60 years ago, whose prayers started it? And as we prayed for peace then, did we realise that our prayers would help to build the Bomb and end the war in a flash – by killing and maiming 300,000 people?

Now we are praying for world peace again. I wonder what new calamities we're about to bring down upon the earth?

Do you understand prayer?

Do you know the difference between the force of prayer and the power of prayer?

I don't think so. For if you did, the earth and its people would not be in such an awful mess – poised on the edge of the ultimate in disaster.

Prayer is the most effective, misused and misunderstood force in the world.

If you allow it, I am going to present to you a new way to pray, a way to save the earth and its people of the future.

Whether you consider yourself an atheist, agnostic or materialist is irrelevant. Terms like those are a way of entertaining yourself and have no real meaning. You are a human being. That means you pray. Everyone prays. You are praying at this moment only you don't realise it. It is that unawareness or ignorance that has brought humanity to the verge of annihilation.

You are praying – emanating an invisible and potentially dangerous force – when you are striving towards an end; when you are excited or depressed, feel threatened or are unhappy. And you pray every moment by wishing and hoping – wishing and hoping that your plans will work out; that what you are trying to do will succeed; that your next baby will be a boy or a girl; that you won't get sick; that you'll be able to keep a date.

You are praying when you want anything.

You also pray every moment by expecting – expecting that what you own will be there when you want it; that your lover still loves you; that death won't trouble you today. You pray when you are being greedy – when you have your eye on the last prawn on the table, or the last drink.

And when you are restlessly impatient, angry or desiring sex, you are praying very intensely.

To exist and survive in this world as a person is an activity of constant prayer. Rays or waves of vital force radiate out from you into the world as continuous projections. The more concentrated and intense you are at any moment the stronger and more forcible are your personal prayer-waves. Sometimes they reach the pitch of violence.

All this would be harmless if the prayer-waves coming out of us were ineffectual as we all seem to imagine. But they are not ineffectual. They are energetically substantive and accumulative. They have been building up since time began and today in their global interaction they form the world's most destructive and diabolical invisible force.

PRAYING FOR SUCCESS

*A*s prayer is the most effective force in the world, and since everyone seeks and prays continuously to not fail, why is there failure in the world?

Failure occurs because success or gain can only come at someone else's expense.

For you to be a successful poet, politician or business person (which means that is your constant prayer) some other poor poet, politician or business person has to fail or lose. There is only so much of everything in the world and that includes success or gain.

The success of the world is represented at any moment by what each of its thousands of millions of people have gained. Only so many can be rich because only so many can be poor. The cake of the world, like the energy of the universe, is only so much at any time. It's determined by what has been extracted from the earth. As the privileged nations take increasing wealth out of the earth, the cake gets bigger, the rich get richer and the poor get poorer.

There would be ample to go round if everyone had only what they need. But because so many have prayed for and grabbed more than they need, it's no longer possible for the original losers to get back their share: somebody like us has already got it.

The 'haves' like you and me who can afford the luxury of praying to be successful poets, politicians or business people, are merely playing or praying among ourselves with someone else's lost share of cake – while they toil or pray for the pitiful success of not starving. That's why success seems so abstract to us: it's lost the reality of an empty belly.

To the super rich of the world we in turn are the poor. The super rich who are few in number but nevertheless keep grabbing the most cake or booty, do not struggle or pray to eat or be successful poets, politicians or business people. The rich pray only to be successful at wielding power by economic force – which is to keep the shareout fixed forever as it is. Their prayer is the mightiest prayer of all. It holds the world together so that all the 'haves' can continue taking and having.

So to succeed in anything, whether as an individual, an organisation or a nation, we have to take from some other person, organisation or nation, somewhere. Which doesn't say a great deal for the way of prayer or way of life that we've devised, does it?

If all our prayers work towards success, how does anyone actually lose?

Because some of us are praying for the success of one thing and others are praying for the success of its opposite. One cancels out the other, or the strongest prayer eventually wins. But it can be quite a drawn-out tussle for all but the super rich, as living shows.

Also, some of us are actually praying for the failure of others, or other things, and the success of praying for another's failure is of course for them to fail. Then there are half-hearted prayers which get overwhelmed by more intense prayers. And so on.

But you'll notice that most of our regular praying, such as that involved in getting you to work each day, succeeds most of the time – as long as it doesn't clash too much with what others want or are praying for. Prayer works – and always towards success – otherwise you couldn't make any arrangements at all.

You are able to pray pretty confidently by making plans to go on holiday on a certain date, and most times you make it. You can usually manage to keep advance appointments and to watch your favourite TV program. You pray to keep your job and generally do – but if you get lax in your praying or someone starts praying against you, you might lose it.

The whole world of circumstances is the meeting of multiple billions of these prayer-waves – psychic forces – which humanity is continuously giving out. Some harmonise and help each other. Some are inconsonant and oppose each other. And some attract each other but at the same time are inconsonant – so two cars collide, a company crashes, someone starves to death on the other side of the earth, or a building full of people gets bombed.

All of this, the uncertainty of living, is the work of the blind force of unconscious, irresponsible personal prayer.

PIOUS PRAYERS

*N*ow we come to the deliberate prayers of all those children (not to mention adults) praying every night and day the world over for someone or other to be blessed or especially favoured; the prayers of you and I praying for a small miracle when we're in a tight spot, and of billions of others praying indiscriminately all around the earth to right the world's apparent ills.

At this point I have to ask you a question, very seriously. Did you really think that all those innocent-sounding prayers could be projected continuously into the world by generation after generation without setting in motion some sort of law of cause and effect? Did you perhaps even venture to assume that if nothing else, they were harmless?

If such prayers are not effective, why does humanity pray? Why has it always prayed? And if its prayers are effective, who said they are only effective of good? Have you ever thought about this?

Here's another very serious question. Do you really think you know what's wrong with the world? – sufficient to take it upon yourself to try to change it for what you think would be better?

And do you trust the judgment of all those others, including the children, who also are praying because they think they know what's wrong or good?

Are you prepared to be answerable in your life for all the changes involved in making the one change you pray for?

Would you pray so easily, and sleep so untroubled, if you knew that the effect of all your prayers – not just the effect you are praying for – would come back on you?

For that is precisely what happens.

All the prayers of the human race – unconscious and deliberate – knit up together. And remember, this has been going on since time began – prayer-waves contending with each other to work themselves out as circumstances in the world, and continuing to do so ages after the generations who prayed them are long forgotten.

The result is that a stupendous ferment of unexhausted prayers, a mighty field of force, has built up around the simplicity of the earth and its people. This field of force is the world.

And now the force of the world has reached flashpoint, disaster point, not for just a few nations as in 1945, but for all nations.

You don't have to believe me. Keep checking the daily news media and listen to the growing public protests of the worried people of the earth. All I'm doing is telling you the cause.

The combined effects of all humanity's praying descends in continuous waves on humanity – disaster after disaster somewhere in the world day after day, but never so close to us all as now. These effects are the condition of the world at any moment – the circumstances in which you and I and the rest of the earth's people must endeavour to live our little lives.

TIME'S ALMOST UP

*W*hat the world is facing today with justified trepidation and a deepening sense of disaster, which will turn to terror, is a mighty moving mountain of undischarged responsibility for all our blind, selfish and irresponsible praying.

The force that went out of us and made the world what it is, has returned to claim its source. It is here. And it's about to come down on us.

Much of what I am now going to say will be unsettling and disturbing. It will linger in you. To the extent that you are real it will keep coming up in your awareness and cause a lot of self-searching.

In what follows I am making a positive statement about life now, and the future of life on earth, but in the present depressed condition of humanity it is likely to be perceived as negative.

The world as we know it is finished. There is going to be an awful wipe-out. Just about all the earth's population will be destroyed. But not quite all. The human race will survive.

The end can come any day. No day is safe any more. The days at least used to be safe before our constant praying for favouritism and peace-from-war – instead of justice for all – produced the technological and biological means of global destruction.

Ever since those inventions, the margin of time has been closing. Time, after all, is only the reducing distance between accountability for what you have received and what you have given. Now, apart from the daily period of waiting, time's up. There is no escape. It's heads down for all of us.

All that can be done in the world has been done.

Whatever is done now will be just another move in the step towards the end. Things can't get better except in the imagination and the daily media. All the peace movements, all the leaders, prime ministers, presidents and armies – even the loftiest and most selfless actions – can't prevent what's coming.

Do you want to argue that what I'm saying isn't true? Do you want to stop reading and try to push the whole thing out of your mind? Or go merrily on your complacent way, imagining it's okay – that someone or something will work it out and save the day?

This is not a bad dream that you're going to wake up from. It's real. Please look at it.

Many people will be dismayed by what I am saying. That is unavoidable. But I want to help you to see and understand what is going on, for it is because you have not faced up, not understood the world – have confused the world with the earth – that you are now frightened or apprehensive. I didn't invent the peril; you don't get dismayed or frightened by fiction. It's the authenticity of the situation, presented without any fantasy of escape, that is dawning on you – penetrating you.

As a spiritual teacher it is my responsibility to reveal to you the truth. I am telling you the truth of the world and what's going to happen – and it may happen any day now.

When you look closely at what I'm saying you'll see it's not so different to what the more reflective people of the earth have been saying for years: if you don't desist you're going to blow us all up. Well, we haven't desisted and I'm telling you it's now too late for the 'if' – the hope.

No Hope

*I*n this world we live on hope. To live in the world we have to – and I have removed the hope. Did you really have any hope before I spoke? Of course not. There's no hope in this world because you're going to die.

Like the world, you can die any day. But you keep yourself from going mad with the thought of this by living in hope, in the fantasy that you'll die in some distant tomorrow. The fact that the world is now about to die too, is really incidental. It's terrifying because it means you've run out of tomorrows, run out of world to escape into.

How can you go on in the world if it's going to end? You go on exactly as you are. Nothing's changed. How did you go on each day before, when you knew you were going to die?

I am not going to give you hope. But I am going to give you more of the truth which is the strength of life.

I have said that the world is going to be destroyed, not the earth. That's very important to remember; because it is the earth, not the world, that you love. The earth will be here; and if you really come to life in the time you've got, you'll be here too.

The earth and the life-forms on it will receive a savage, punishing blow. The earth too has to pay a penalty, as it's already doing, for the selfishness of the intelligent life – us – that came out of it. We humans are of the earth; we are the original life-form of pure reflective intelligence on earth. But out of our ignorance – our wilful disregard for life – came the destructive human self-conscious intelligence that created the world.

The earth is responsible for us as a mother is responsible for her child. If the child is irresponsible or unloving, the mother will suffer in some way.

Our tremendous free-wheeling intelligence is the problem. We are very clever, very smart children. But right from the start we have been takers. With our unfeeling intelligence and selfish greed we took from the mother without consideration until a third of her was reduced to desert for which we cleverly blamed the elements; and at the same time we took from each other until half of us were starving or impoverished, for which we again cleverly blamed everything but ourselves.

Without let-up the mother and the life on earth continue to be denuded and deprived by our rapacious intelligence. At every level of existence human intelligence has demonstrated greed and exploitation using the excuse and euphemism of progress.

Progress is essential, says human intelligence. Is it? Or is it only essential when you're running from something?

The trouble is: we got it wrong to start with. Our intelligence should have been the servant; that is, it should have served some real value. But the human race has had no real values – nothing of worth that ever lasted. And with nothing to serve but its shifting self-interest, the smart servant became the clever master.

Today we still serve nothing of value – only progress and convenience. What do you serve, give your life to, that is not of your own? What is the world devoted to? We simply don't know what to do with our intelligence. We're stuck. We're going towards self-destruction and we can't stop.

Can you believe it? You've got to believe it. Keep reading the newspapers: it's actually happening. All we do is fight and oppose, be for or against, vote this way or that, and hope for a final compromise. That's all human intelligence knows.

Will you try a different way? Put your human intelligence second? Will you give life itself a chance?

HUMAN ART AND REAL ART

*I*s there anything human intelligence has created that is worth saving in this world? What in the world is worth preserving?

Would you make a mental list please?

Persons? If you think certain persons are worth saving then why does everybody die – and many of them very young, too? Life on earth – which is still the master of death – doesn't rate persons valuable at all as our intelligence tries to. Life is indeed valuable. That's why it's always here. But persons come and go; as you and I will.

The person you are is not the reality you are. The infinitely more intelligent reality behind your person is what I endeavour to address. The person is what you and I project into the world and give a name to. My person is called Barry Long. The person you are is what performs and reacts in the world. The person – every person who ever lived – is what has brought us to this awful point.

Art? Our intelligence has murdered art. The art we think of as art is a last pitiful remnant of the great art that once was life on earth itself – the great art of being a trouble-free human being – before the self-conscious person took over.

Why do so few of the earth's population value what we call 'art', even in our own intelligent society? Why is there so much room in art for posturing and humbug? Because it is not art. It's just all we've got left, all we can muster at the end of an inglorious era. A few paintings, statues, texts, ruins is all we've got to show for five thousand years of intelligent civilisation, of creeping westernisation.

And what will we leave of our art today apart from the nuclear bomb, biological weapons, missiles and other death-dealing achievements? Our dance, music, film, paintings, sculpture, words? Are they memorable? Are they alive – like the great art of producing really intelligent men and women? Or does our art just manage to give a temporary living to the few who try so hard to give it life?

Is our art truly worth preserving as the creative spirit itself? Or have we debased the creative living spirit that was Man – the great art on earth that once was us – and replaced it with human intelligence which is no more the living spirit than its fruitless offspring, the sterile spaceship, computer and nuclear reactor.

What about ideas? – such as those that developed the means of creating electricity, space travel and our high-tech, high-con society? Perhaps you think they're worth saving? That's because you can't see life beyond progress, beyond the intelligence that produced the means of total destruction.

Our ideas do not serve anything of real value; they

all go in one direction – away from life or the earth, towards death, the nuclear bomb or the cultured germ. We can't get rid of the bomb, or its cultured partner, no matter how hard we try, because our technology will invent a better device – a simpler, easier one; a do-it-yourself more instant one. It can't be avoided. That's the way we think. That's progress.

Hoping to improve the world we develop wonderful ideas; and invariably they contribute to greater competition, rivalry, political opportunism, fear and exploitation – whether of space, nature or people. All because we don't know what to serve.

Our intelligence is out of control. The rich have won. The share-out stays fixed. In winning at the expense of others we have lost it all.

OUR SCIENTIFIC GENIUS
WILL BE THE MEANS

*A*nything worth preserving is of the earth and not of our civilisation. Our achievements are completely expendable, as were those of all previous civilisations. Nothing of any consequence has survived any of them – except the earth and the life on it, which is all that will survive of this civilisation.

Your dismay and attempt to disbelieve what I'm saying is because you happen to be at the end of this civilisation. Life is the same at the end of every civilisation. And of course it's almost impossible for you – as it was for all the others at the end of their civilisations – to imagine that your world is finished. Would you please look at this. See whether it is true. For I can only point out the truth. You have to recognise it for yourself.

All previous civilisations were corrupt like ours – futile attempts by man to create a world of his own on the already perfect earth. And all eventually destroyed themselves, or unsuspectingly allowed themselves to be destroyed, through what they considered to be their finest achievement.

In our case the means of destruction will be our scientific genius, our clever intellectual materialism.

Nothing of previous civilisations do we consider to be of sufficient value to retain as our way of life. Because nothing in those civilisations – like nothing in ours – was of any real value. The bits and pieces we keep around are not a way of life. Whatever is of real value – once you find it – you live. You don't shut it up in museums or books; and you don't study it. You simply live it.

There are no scholars, professionals or professors of life or love – life or love being the true value of life on earth. All scholars and practising students are of the world and they study the things of the world. They are as unconsciously lacking life and real love as the things they study. Likewise the world's workers and its wealthy players who have lost touch with the power within. They are as unconscious as the world they toil and play in.

Life can't be studied. You can't study life on earth because you are life on earth. You can only love life and be life. What people study are life-forms and for-mulas, not life. A form of life is not life itself.

THE WORLD'S BOOBY PRIZE

*O*ur main problem is that we have given ourselves to the world. Each of us has given great
slices of our precious life to the drudgery of years and
years of studying and learning subjects that have nothing to do with the fulfilment we yearn for.

And after even more years of practising what we've
studied and learned, we settle for the world's booby
prize – experience.

Experience certainly makes the work or occupation
easy or easier – and indeed easier to get a better-paying
though more demanding job. But would anyone in their
right mind regard 'easy' as a substitute for the delight

of continuous, spontaneous creative self-expression?

Each of us is born with a *unique* creative talent which soon gets buried under the irksome grind of having to study, learn and practise. And when at last we become proficiently experienced, we're probably qualified to teach others how to become as busy, unfulfilled and fundamentally frustrated as we are.

Please let us look at this together.

Why does every skilled trade, craft and professional activity in the world have to be studied and learned? Why must you study and practise to be a singer, painter, dancer, writer, musician, doctor, carpenter, teacher or any other form of self-expression?

Why as an infant did you have to start learning lessons at school to prepare you for adult life so many years ahead? And for more years to have to go through the inevitable strain and anxieties of being tested, examined intellectually and compared competitively with others?

The answer is: because the immense effort and years of learning and practising to master or understand anything – including school subjects – attaches you to the world, and ensures that you sacrifice your natural creativity for the rewards of experience.

The natural talent everyone is born with is an ability to contribute something of value to life on earth. The discovery and practical expression of this is the ultimate joy of living.

But right from the start we are taught through studying and learning to concentrate on worldly goals with the result that few ever enjoy enduring pleasure and fulfilment in their daily work.

The world is a hard master. Once you are experienced it will keep you in drudgery out of fear for as long as it can. But if you pursue your natural talent and stick to it you'll break through the fear and be complete in what you do – even if it means less money and less esteem from others still scared by the world.

The extraordinary thing is that you don't need experience to do what you love doing; inspiration just comes naturally.

If you give the world your entire life, which most people are doing today, the world will short-change you. Nothing is more short-lived or problematical than success. The most powerful and successful people worry, feel unloved, misunderstood and get depressed. No one who has learned to be anything in this world is happy for long.

The world of experience is filled with promises. The hope is for fulfilment; the reality is passing success then discontent or frustration. Many, if not all, very experienced people are trapped for years in very important worldly positions while yearning desperately for self-expression.

Some study religion and unsuccessfully try to practise the rules. Some study crime and learn how to successfully break the rules. Others become politicians and learn that the highest altruistic motives are doomed to be drowned in compromise, or defeated by the vested interests of the powerful.

Most of the people do what the world expects of them – and consequently experience spasmodic satisfaction, much searching, changing, boredom and trying to cope with the emotional frustration of their selves and others.

Every day the world requires men and women to make even greater sacrifices of their life and time. How much of your life have you had to spend learning? Aren't you learning now – struggling to break through the world in some way or other? The exhausting effort is why you seldom feel really alive – and why so often you long to be allowed to be your natural self.

To be successful, the young are forced to study into their mid-twenties, thirties and even forties – or they just give up. But you can't just give up or drop out. The world won't let you. It's everybody's rat-race. In one way or another the sacrifice must be made to the insatiable appetite of the world – if not in time, then in pain, boredom or tears.

Have you noticed how many teenagers and adults don't know what occupation to follow? What they want to do with their lives? And how many realise in later life that they made the wrong choices, not only in regard to work but particularly in relationships?

All because we've been taught to put enjoyment of the world before our natural enjoyment of life.

The world these days teaches the young to please

themselves. No one really has the time or knowledge to help them discover their inner worth – because all who try are also unwitting victims of the world.

Can things get better? Not a chance. The only saving grace is that each new generation believes it was always like this – that the air and oceans are polluted, that you mustn't leave your door unlocked, that it's unsafe to walk out alone at night, that public toilets have padlocked steel boxes for the needles of drug users, that a terrorist attack may kill or maim you any day, and so on and so on.

There's not much time any more in our global society for enjoying life on earth. The looking forward to holidays and weekends is a sure sign of that.

Take love. Everyone on earth today has learned how to love. The result is that when the time comes for them to really love they have to unlearn what the world has taught them – and that is the pain, the dying to the world that you feel when your lover fails you or your heart is broken. Or the sheer boredom that accompanies repetitive sex without love, without life.

When you return to the love of life – which is your natural talent – and put that first, you can love wherever you will without complications or problems.

If only someone had taught us differently to begin with.

IT TAKES TRAGEDY TO CHANGE US

*I*n witnessing and being totally involved in the catastrophic tragedy of the end of the world, man and woman will undergo an enormous change in consciousness.

The unprecedented experience will disintegrate all the old patterns of mind, incendiarise and purge the human psyche of its shaky foundations, and transform self-consciousness on earth.

The personal self in self-consciousness, with all its false notions and troublesome ways, will be obliterated, leaving the survivors in an unimaginable state of pure consciousness.

No class of people will be left out of the devastation. No politicians, industrialists, royalty, financiers, generals, scientists or workers will remain to imagine and discuss the carnage from the protected position of bystanders. Every individual will be the battlefield of personal soul-raking tragedy.

Why? Why in the purpose of things is such horrific devastation and suffering necessary?

Because only personal tragedy changes us. Of all the tragedy that has ever been in the world, it has never affected the majority before.

Consequently, humanity has always lived off the imagined security of the majority – the world – and has changed very little. This time, however, engulfed in total tragedy which leaves no escape, no room for intellectual discussion or fantasy, the survivors will change. The world will be literally blown out of them.

From our worldly point of view, it would seem that these men and women will know enormous personal suffering for a long time. But in their new impersonal consciousness they will not see it that way. They will not recover and embrace the world again, as we do now when tragedy strikes here and there. None will ever again be the man or woman they were before. Each will be a creature of higher intelligence.

It is impossible for the human mind to imagine what the new life on earth is to be. We cannot conceive of the earth without the world. All our imaginings are of the world, of our self-consciousness, and are not true. But by simply reading what I have to say, and not employing your worldly faculties of thinking or reasoning, you will hear the truth; and you may notice a subtle elevation of recognition within. It is the world alone that prevents you from hearing the truth and being what you really are.

As the world within and without vanishes, the survivors will be in contact with the power I'm endeavouring to reveal in you now. This power, guiding from within, will be intensely real and immediate because it will no longer have to come through the deadening barrier of the world. Helped and directed by the power, the survivors will be intelligent and responsible – since at last they will have discovered something of enduring value.

Each will have discovered the reality of life within – his and her reality.

Surely everyone already knows that they are life? Isn't it implicit in being alive?

People are aware of being alive but are not conscious of being life. If they were they'd realise immortality – life without the world – and be free forever of fear and doubt.

Every living thing, including your own body, is a form of life – and all forms must pass away, die. We've become so used to living and seeing things die that we have lost the consciousness of life, through identifying with death as an end.

Life is a far more subtle consciousness than the awareness of living and being alive. Living and being alive depend for confirmation on the physical senses which are mortal. But life is immortal. And the realisation of life itself, the immediate consciousness of immortality, is what is coming.

So really, *the end of the world is only depressing while the individual holds on to his or her mortality.*

After the end of the world, everything worth preserving in man and woman and the rest of the species will continue. The survivors will love, serve and know life – as men and women have longed to do, but have not been able to do, for thousands of years. They will be in continuous intimate contact with life within, and with the earth and life around them, as one living organism.

The survivors will have an enlightened aversion for the past and retain practically no memory of it. They will not long for what has been. They will know that it was the past – that which we defended as our way of life and allowed to happen – that decimated the earth and the life on it.

They will have no sympathy at all for the likes of us, no affection for us. *They will regard us as the unforgivable barbarians who wantonly and wilfully deflowered the earth.*

And if any person like us should reappear, the world will be summarily obliterated from them, just as it was from the earth and the survivors.

The men and women who survive will have nothing to learn, nothing to study and distract them; nothing that would allow another world like ours to build up again. They will have learned the only lesson to be learned from living, which we never learned: that to lose contact with the power within by trying to create another world with human intelligence is inevitable disaster.

As the conscious surviving part of future life on earth the survivors will have access to the creative genius of life – as distinct from our much-prized human ingenuity. The creativity will be directed from within by the creative spirit itself. No longer will they have anything to do with progress. They will have discovered a real value to serve, the supreme genius of life. And their ideas will work for life, for good, not for death-dealing devices or personal gain.

DYING FOR LIFE

*H*aven't you felt for most of your life that your views and opinions should be respected? That in some small way you're entitled to have a say or a hand in determining your destiny – by voting and making decisions? Or that at least you should be considered or consulted?

Well, you're right. The final responsibility is yours. It is your world after all.

Incredible, isn't it? – that it should all finally depend, or descend on you.

Yet every one of us feels that we're somehow important; that our life must have some purpose beyond just living and dying. Many have been inspired by the idea or notion of Jesus dying for the world. Dare you put yourself on the same level? Dare you not?

You are the hope of life on earth. That's what it comes down to.

In the time we've got, let's get it right, or more right. I am not asking you to join a peace movement, to change your religion, to make any kind of protest or public announcement, to believe in anything or even to agree with me. I'm just asking you to take responsibility for being a human being on this earth.

You may think you're already taking this responsibility. But what you've been taking responsibility for is the person you are, not the being you are; and no overt action by any person can change what is coming – the world's confrontation with its own reality, the truth of its own making.

In the time that is left the only change that can be effective for good has to happen in you, the individual. You have to change your person, transform it – metamorphose like the butterfly. You can do this only by making and continuing to make the ultimate personal sacrifice – to willingly surrender the person you are on behalf of the greater good.

You have to be, not a martyr in the physical sense, but a super being in the real sense. And you've got to do it alone. No one else is going to listen or hear – only you.

You can't leave it to fate because fate's against you. It's fate, Nemesis itself, that's coming.

You can't even leave it to God, Jesus, the Buddha or any other divinity. God, Jesus, the Buddha, the spirit of mankind, can and definitely will save you, the being. There's no doubt about that: you are already saved, because only the body dies. But God can't save the world of persons from its fate, or the world from itself.

Yet you can give the earth a new kind of human being.

Will you?

WHY BOTHER?

*W*hy should anybody bother to change when the end is coming anyway?

Because first, when you change or transform your person while still alive, your life becomes increasingly easy and finally unimaginably more fulfilling.

And secondly, because the state of survival (which I'm going to describe) is determined by the individual's degree of self-knowledge.

Self-knowledge depends on knowing your self. How much you know your self you can see in your own experience by your separation from the person – the troublesome *self* that develops in every body from birth.

You are going to die anyway, and perhaps that will happen before the world calamity occurs. In that case, the same principle of self-knowledge applies. The real intelligence you are – and you are far more really intelligent than your mind can know – determines the inner depth of survival your intelligence gravitates to.

Real intelligence *at its swiftest* is impersonal. It is not attached to anyone or any thing. But in truth – which means death, which means life – there are degrees of impersonality. And again that depends on separation or transformation of the personal self while living.

The question is, how do you recognise the person or self that you have to face – then separate from, and ideally, transform?

THE SPOILER

THE PERSON

The personal self is responsible for the degeneration of the quality of life on earth and the
current dilemma of the world.

It starts developing in everybody from the moment
of birth. It is a living reflection, a copy, of the environ-
ment, society and world that the child is born into. The
person slowly gathers its values and later its opinions
and beliefs from those multiple shifting and fragmented
influences.

From infancy to adulthood the differences keep
growing due to experience, and the person becomes
increasingly divided. Moreover, as no two people have

identical impressions of any experience there is almost complete diversity between persons.

This leaves the individual person basically unsure of itself and isolated. In other words, insecure. And its aim throughout is to embrace anything that provides it with a sense of being a seemingly whole entity. The personal self manages this most effectively by identifying with such strong universal beliefs as religion, nationalism and politics – together with the moral attitudes of the generation and the customs of the times.

War and tragedy, in particular, temporarily binds together all the persons affected. But once the crisis passes, the persons inevitably start disagreeing and fighting among themselves at the domestic, ethnic, religious or nationalistic level.

As the person is primarily concerned with itself, it cannot avoid putting self-interest first – what it owns and its own beliefs and opinions. At every level the person is selfish.

The strength of drive behind the person's selfishness is the continuous frustration and inner conflict of never having been fulfilled or satisfied for long or having achieved anything that lasts. The one exception is its own self-satisfying image of itself; and the reverse self-satisfaction of discontent, depression, self-hate and moodiness that it imposes even on loved ones.

The wilful and forceful core of the person is self, and out of that arises the person's selfish nature. Try as the person might to be kind, to do good, to bring about worthwhile change or reform, the effort invariably ends in failure, disappointment, misunderstandings, destructive criticism and at best, soggy compromise.

Self consists of conflict – all the emotional hurts and frustrations that the person has suffered since birth. These emotions slowly join up to finally form an inner entity of self-doubt, fear and dread of being exposed for the phony it is. The personal self's defence is big talk, lying, bravado, forceful argument, cunning – and blaming and accusing others.

That's the world of persons: everyone pulling in different directions, wanting and praying for different and opposite things, until temporarily united by tragedy, war or a good idea that in the long haul will turn out faulty and create the very conditions it was supposed to heal or change.

Most of the time you suppress the mass of insecurity that is your person. But faced with loss or threat the person usually takes over and causes negative actions and reactions, especially worry, self-doubt, anger and dread of the future.

Selfish derives from self. And ridding ourselves of self is the only way to effect a fundamental change. We can't change the world. But in changing our self we can make a surprising difference.

What is Good?

Everybody's enjoyment of life is spoiled by their person – particularly when life is felt to be good. At those times, something contrary usually seems to happen and ruin the sense of contentment or success. The reason is that the personal self has risen from within and is trying to share in what is good. But as the self is an insecure emotional bundle of unhappiness and negativity, its invasion wrecks the good feeling.

On the wider worldly scene, the collective selves of nations and cultures praying against each other keep humanity from realising that great and wonderful ideal of 'peace on earth, goodwill towards all'.

For such peace and goodwill to ever manifest, life on earth has to be freed of our ingrained irresponsible way of thinking, and our selfishness. Being selfish we can't help but project our selves into every thing we do. We know of no alternative because we don't know what is good.

What is good? I ask you now.

As if you don't know.

We all know: life is good.

In times of tragedy you suddenly realise it again. But soon you forget it and get on with your personal life – until the next time. You don't seem to realise the lessons of tragedy – whether it's the death of a loved one, your own downfall, or mass slaughter – that life, the good, is always here in you. And that at any moment you are undeniably life on earth.

Life on earth is good; or it was until the humanity created another sort of life – living in the world. As the world spread over the earth, awareness of life, the good, diminished; and living as comfort and convenience got easier.

So today living is fairly easy with its scientific gadgetry and enlightened dole queues; but life, the enriching and revivifying 'good' is that much harder to find. And any day now, as the world finally demonstrates its crowning achievement in gadgetry or living, there won't be much life around at all.

But life is still good, isn't it? It was still good before the world began strangling it – and it is still good beneath the strangulation we all experience.

HUMAN NATURE AND OUR TRUE NATURE

*R*idding ourself of the world doesn't mean trying to get rid of the external world – which we can't do anyway. The external world will do that of itself.

The individual's task is more simple: to discard the inner rubbish by shedding the wilful worldly person that has taken possession and controlled most of the living life. This will reveal the true nature, the being, underneath.

Your true nature is not human nature. Your true nature is of the earth, not of the world. The earth is what we came out of through the mater, the matter, the mother, and so the nature of the earth with all its endless beauty and immediacy is our true nature.

Human nature is the worldly nature that has buried our true nature and brought us to this wretched predicament. No particular person or society is to blame. We, as personal links in an endless chain of humanity, are all responsible.

The cumulative effects of human nature, the legacy of all generations, is reflected in the ugliness and brutality of the world at any time. The world is the mirror of human nature.

The immediate task is to free this planet, its people and ourselves as much as can be accomplished in the time we've got, from the cumulative effects of our misguided prayers and personal prayer-waves of wishing, wanting and hoping. What the world prays for is what we get. That is our fate, and in a world of persons where everyone is praying for something different, the fate is eventual disaster.

We must not go on adding to the mass of that incurably selfish personal praying. And we have to be sure that our prayers today don't bring misfortune tomorrow. In other words, you and I have to reverse the work of the force of selfish prayer through the power of right prayer.

THE POWER OF PRAYER

RIGHT PRAYER

*T*he way of prayer I'm now going to present to you is a way to help save the earth and its people of the future. By helping you to understand prayer and the reality behind what's happening in the world, I'm putting you in touch with new power within your being, power deep in the unconscious, that is now rising and ready to be released for good.

To pray rightly you must not pray for anything to happen or not happen in the world.

You must not pray by asking for the sick or troubled to be made well or untroubled. You must not ask to reverse the condition of anyone; or pray for anyone to receive anything. Praying for people like that only transfers misfortune from one place to another.

If prayers work to help a person (and they sometimes do because all prayer works towards success) you are taking something from someone else in the world somewhere – whose condition then worsens. That might be yourself, for remember, your prayers come back on you. It's not uncommon for someone close to a sick person to also become ill after the person has recovered or died. Multiply this effect by a billion prayers a day and you get the poverty, misery and suffering that never leaves the world.

Praying for people releases force. What the afflicted in this world need is not more force, but more power – more life and love. Power is all positive; whereas force is positive and negative, and thus creates the world of opposites, the world of pain and gain.

When you pray for a particular person to be saved, you leave someone else out. So you upset the balance of life and create the condition of injustice in living that requires someone to lose for another to gain. You make the world stronger and contribute to the unhappiness of life on earth. It must be that everyone is blessed; not just someone whom you think should be.

To pray rightly you must resist the urge to pray for particular people to be saved. Instead, simply hold the image/knowledge of them, or your love of them, unmoving within you. Don't think about them; that is, don't let the image move. Keep the corners of your mouth up. Smile a little; if you are in touch with your love within, this will happen naturally. Don't allow yourself to think about the past, your sadness or loneliness; and don't cry. Any of that will detract from the power. Stay with the image/knowledge and love.

By resisting the urge to pray for a person, by not using force which is the way of the world, the power of life and love is released within you. And because you are holding the knowledge or love (and rightly containing your concern for them) the power will go to them. They will be comforted in some way even though their external circumstances may not appear to change; for all things must die as some things must fail. But you will have released the power of good into existence uncontaminated by personal desire.

The power of prayer, unlike the force of prayer, will not deprive another in order to heal or comfort the one you are concerned for. The power will go wherever it is needed in the world without having any injurious, negative effect.

And don't try to pray for 'everyone'.

You and I are not vast enough, not just and wise enough, loving, humble and selfless enough, to pray for the earth and all its people. To take responsibility for such a prayer you would have to be life itself, the power itself. And then there would be no need for the prayer, or the pray-er.

Do you see this? With our self-projecting, self-selected prayers we wrap the goodness of the earth, and those who come and go on it, in a short-sighted, unjust world.

But it is possible to be in a continuous subconscious state of right prayer by being grateful *every moment* for the good in your life. This is a natural emanation – though not a normal one – once you've given up personal force for the impersonal power.

Pray as often as you can without any image in your mind. Pray to be one with life, one with the good, one with the earth, one with the source, one with God. But you must match this in your external life with a sincere endeavour to rid yourself of anger, impatience, resentment and negative feelings. They are all personal.

Find the life within you. Don't think about it: sense it. You are alive, aren't you? – so life must be there. Compared with your personal feelings and thoughts life is extremely subtle and usually overwhelmed. Nevertheless find it. Sense it. Be it.

Stop giving yourself to the world. Give yourself to life. Sink into the good of it, for the good within you *is* life.

The power will then work in you and through you. You will find you are truly serving people in the world. And you will know that you are coming to life.

The power is with you – if you give up the force.

PRAYERS OF FREEDOM

*T*he error of the world is in you and me. Free the world of your error and you free it of yourself. Free it of yourself and you create a little bit of space for love and rightness to surface in the world and work for good.

To free the world or anything of yourself is to help to heal it. Love and rightness are already there ready to work on any condition of sickness, poverty or misery – once you create the necessary space in your being by getting yourself out of the way.

Pray like this for the starving and suffering of the world:

'I free you of my anger, my greed, my thoughtlessness and my thoughtfulness in wanting to change things for you without giving my life to you.

'I free you of my opinions about what caused your condition. I free you of my interest in reading about and viewing your misery, in seeing your emaciated bodies and hearing of your suffering, while my belly is full.'

The people you feed with belly-food today will be hungry again tomorrow. Or if they're not, some others will be. All are suffering from the same disease, the same condition of the world – the lack of life and love in you and me.

In praying like this, you don't have to do anything, take any overt action or change your life. To do so, or think you should, is the usual reactive self-ish way which will only perpetuate error in the world.

This way of prayer is new. Such prayers have not been said before, or if they have, no one has ever really seen them as statements of their own personal ignorance.

The remarkable thing is that the prayers are for you. They are not going to help anyone else directly. As you see the truth of the prayers, you'll be changed within. Not that you'll know. It will just happen. And because you've become more real and intelligent, the world will be a slightly better place.

The change however depends on you actually *seeing* the truth of what you're saying – and realising that this is not about others but about the person you are. The absence of this self-knowledge – the lack of real intelligence in men and women – has created the appalling conditions the prayers describe.

In continuing to pray for the starving and suffering, say:

'I free you of my ignorance in thinking that I was really sorry for you or that I had helped you by sending money or food. For that money or food, which I didn't need, must have come from someone else – from yourself, perhaps, or from those who must starve tomorrow.

How did I come to have so much when you have nothing? You weren't always hungry. Who took it from you and gave it to me?

'All the prayers of the privileged certainly worked against you, didn't they? Made us rich and you hungry. Your prayers must have been too simple, too natural, and you lost out. Now it looks as though we've been too smart and prayed ourselves into a far greater impoverishment than yours.

'I know now that I must help to end the condition that causes your poverty and hunger. I must give up my self, give up my selfish prayers and this foolish, thoughtless, thinking person who thought that misery was natural on the earth.'

Pray to free the world of your personal self.

'I free the world of my prayers and my wanting, wishing and hoping. I pray for nothing in the world. I want nothing from the world except what I am given and what I earn.

'I free the world of my notions of what is good and what should be changed.

'I free you – everyone and everything – from any emotional demands I have put on you. I let the emotion in me go, knowing that love never leaves; that finally all persons and things depart, but never my love.'

The strength of life, of love, is its power to keep giving – giving of itself, not holding on to anything. What have I got to give? Only what my person would hold.

'I hold on to nothing that anyone has said about me or done to me in the past.

'I free you from inside me where I've been holding you a prisoner in my dim, fearing world. If you come back to try to make me hold on to you with resentment, envy or wanting, I pray that I might have the strength of life to let you go again in love.'

Pray to be free of the pressure of the world.

'I have no quarrel with the world. I know it is cruel, violent and difficult. But at least I know where I stand and so I will not be surprised by what the world does to me.

'I live, work and perform in the world. But I do not love the world. I love life and the earth. And in that love I am immortal.'

Don't try to exclude the world from your life for that will only create resistance and add more pressure. You live in this world. You helped to make it. You just can't disown it or get out of it. Do what you must in the world, but don't be confused by it. Give it its due, but not more. Don't be deceived by it. And don't add to it by trying to change it. Change yourself instead.

Transform yourself by being more loving, more patient and aware. Die to your self daily for the power. Help others who are receptive, and especially your children, to understand the difference between life and the world, between power and force.

See yourself as responsible for life and the earth every moment – not only when you feel like it or have the time. Don't hurt the earth or its life-forms any more than you have to. Yet don't feel guilty for what you may have done. Make a fresh start now. The earth forgives our transgressions.

Be of good cheer. Life is now. Life goes on.

A PRAYER FOR LIFE

*P*ray to be one with life and love.
　　'I love. I love life. I love being alive but not at the expense of life or love.

'Because I love life I love many things or some things; but there are things I do not love and do not even think about. As all things are in life, and that life is in me now, I pray that I may love life more, that I may know it more within me, and in this way reach all things that may need more life and love.'

Teach your children to pray with their being and not with their thoughts. Show them that their being is inside their body in the place where they love mummy and daddy. Join them in silently giving thanks every day for all the good things you and they have. Teach them that the good they acknowledge from the place of love brings more love.

Pray by giving thanks at all times; in the bus or train, or while you are walking. You can't run out of the good in your life to give thanks for.

Be grateful while you are making love – and you won't make trouble.

Allow the life, the wonder, to swell in you.

Don't be concentrated. Smile a little. Be open. Be easy. Be empty.

Be loving. Be giving.

Above all, live what you pray.

THE MOST POWERFUL PRAYER

*T*he most powerful prayer is the simplest. Everyone without exception has said this prayer at some time in their life.

The time and the prayer might have been forgotten. But the prayer was uttered. And uttered with a heartfelt urgency that the usual beseeching prayer seldom has.

Beseeching prayer is asking for something.

The most powerful prayer is giving – giving thanks to the unnameable.

Usually this prayer is uttered in an automatic and largely unconscious way, such as when we've just escaped a situation threatening death, ruin or the loss of someone we love. 'Thank God,' we say.

Such thanks may undoubtedly have momentary fervency. But the impulse is still based on getting – having been saved from a devastating situation. (It's not that the prayer of thanks is wasted in the vaster way of things in which all fervent thanks contribute to the good of the whole. It's that the gratitude is of such short duration that it does little to further the consciousness of the pray-er.)

The simplest and most powerful prayer is the one in which you continually give heartfelt thanks for what you've been given in your living life.

'Thank you, thank you, thank you,' is the prayer. However, the second person singular is more intimate, appropriate and divinely natural once you get the idea. Thus, 'I love thee. Thou art beautiful, thou art beauty, thou art all.'

This is giving without getting.

Indeed, you are giving thanks for what you have and are receiving in your life. But it's not about any particular thing. It's about the whole of your life. You are simply grateful. You are thankful that you are able to give thanks. You are thankful that that which you are thanking is there – even though you could never describe it or want to.

Everyone has something to be thankful for. Everyone has some good in their life. But it is human nature to focus for the most part on difficulties and problems, and not on the good.

The extraordinary thing is that the more we pause to acknowledge the good, the more the problems and difficulties disappear, or are soon solved.

It's all a question of consciousness. It takes consciousness to be conscious of the good; and unconsciousness to be absorbed in problems and difficulties.

In those moments of heartfelt prayer, when you can't help giving thanks to the unnameable source of all good, you are truly holy, truly being.

Without thought or intention, pour out your being in gratitude as the bird pours out its being in song.

LOVE

THE STRANGEST IMPERATIVE

*L*ove is the strangest imperative on the planet; strange because we really don't understand it, and an imperative because we can't help but seek it, long for it and try to pursue it all our life.

But what we don't and can't realise is that love is always here. In trying to understand love at any level we overlook the reality of love and mislead ourselves with concepts and notions of love that can never be the real thing.

The difficulty is our human nature and its agency, the human mind. The mind always has a question. It wants answers so that it can know something.

But it is impossible to know love. You can only love love. And when that love of love is deep enough to have transformed your human nature and your mind, you then *are* love. But still you won't know love. You can only know what is separate from you. When you *are* love there's no separation, no distinction, so no knowing.

Nevertheless you are then the *knowledge* of love. In the knowledge or being of love there is no more to know about love, life, truth, death or God; no more questions, no more doubt.

By comparison, knowing anything leads to another question which is a form of doubt. A good example of this is science. Irrespective of what science discovers or knows it always has another question – the insatiable drive to know more. So it is with everybody, particularly in respect of love.

What is this love beyond understanding, beyond the grasp of the mind?

It is life.

So beyond your mind you are life. And when you *real*-ise life you realise what you are.

Life is immortal, not mortal like the mind. Life is in every living thing so unlike the mind it is not individual, personal or particular. Life is always here, wherever here may be; because you are always here. And life does not change, move or waver. Only life-forms change and disappear. But life which animates them goes on unaffected.

Every human being loves life. All endeavour to survive – unless the burden of their human nature is so intolerable that they destroy their own form, their own body. Even so, the life they are is unaffected.

Life is the mystery behind the whole of existence – behind living and death.

You in your reality are that mystery.

And like mystery, there's just no end to Thee.

LOVE FOR ANOTHER

*L*ove for another is the search for love in form, in a body – their body and your own.

As love at every level is an imperative, it is the search for love that drives us all on. Love, as the old saying goes, makes the world go round.

Love is immortal life and we are compelled by the world to try to find it in mortal bodies. This search for love inevitably ends in frustration, heartache, disenchantment or sorrow – since the loved one or the lover must one day leave or die.

It seems so unfair. But is it?

When anybody we love dies or leaves us we are

distressed because while loving them we became attached to them. We attached ourselves emotionally to their body and to the expectation of their continued presence. When the body disappears there is a hole, a vacuum, in our emotions or feelings.

The pleasure of loving and being loved then turns to sorrow. Our emotions writhe and the mind races to attempt to fill the vacuum by trying to understand what has happened. To no avail. The distress and suffering go on until the emptiness is filled by the endless distractions of living, or by the love of someone new.

But why does it happen? Is there a purpose?

The purpose is to show us that love centred on any object is doomed – as all things must pass away or die. The misconception has been going on since time began. But due to our mind and human nature we've lost the intelligence to see the fact.

Moreover, we've lost the intelligence to realise the truth that what we love is life, not living, and that we are life and can never die.

And when we see or hear that thousands of people have died in one mighty terrorist act of indiscriminate violence, we are devastated, shocked beyond belief. For in our ignorance we regard each *body* as life and the event is seen as an incredible destruction of precious life. Also, because the world is a mirror of our selves, we perceive in the disaster our own mortality and hopeless position as a mortal body.

But the reality is that the life in all those people is indeed precious and has not been destroyed at all. It is simply our futile human expectations that have been thwarted and ruptured.

And for good reason. For life is all-intelligent and all-compassionate – as we really are. And life will not leave us to calcify and suffer in our own mortal ignorance of life and death. So life, our reality, repeatedly exposes humanity to loss and tragedy as the only way of eventually awakening us to our true nature and bringing us to life.

The intelligence of life is as vast, profound and incomprehensible as life itself.

Life is behind and in every living thing. When life withdraws, the thing dies. When life partly withdraws, the thing loses its strength and vitality; gets or looks sick. When life almost fully withdraws, the living thing hovers near death.

Life is behind the healthy lustre of living things. Life is behind the night that rejuvenates the bodies wearied and drained from the effort of daily living. Life is behind the infinite variety and beauty of all living things. Life is the architect and creator of all.

Life is behind the regularity of the seasons. The seasons depend upon the position of the sun, so life is behind the sun. And as the rest of the stars need a human brain to apprehend them, life is behind the entire universe and the brain.

Life, like love on earth, is all.

THE SURVIVORS

A New and Different Time

I will now say more about the time after the end of the world, and the survivors. I speak of life in a different time, life free of the complication of the world. Time in the world is sluggish and tedious as everybody knows. But time devoid of the world is so swift as to be immediate, and therefore is incomprehensible to us who live in the world.

At the end of the world, the few survivors will be in this new time. The world will have been extinguished from their perception by the sheer terror of having been directly involved in this unprecedented tragedy. They will perceive life in a new light.

In describing the new state in what follows I realise I'm attempting the unspeakable – which means 'impossible of being expressed in words'. Of course such a disaster itself is unspeakable so it's not surprising there are no words for it.

However, I have to use words or concepts relating to our own worldly time and perception.

Words and concepts cannot in themselves convey true meaning. They invariably provoke imagination, speculation and questions. But in the new time of the survivors there's none of that. Everything, as you will see, is exactly as it is.

The way for us to receive a true reflection of what's being said is to get the *idea* behind the words. This only requires a simple degree of intelligence, somewhat similar to the purified intelligence of the survivors.

Getting the idea means simply reading the words through without pausing for thought or reflection.

That doesn't mean you cannot pause and *look* at what is being said. But it does mean that you can't think about it, that is, you can't allow your mind to move back into what you've heard before or forward in speculation.

Just read what is there. And let your intelligence, which is deeper than your mind, inform you word-lessly.

Their Amazing Vision

With the deadening and distorting world removed from the perception of the survivors, they will see the earth as it really is.

As it really is, the earth is an ethereal reality. It *is* that ethereality now and every moment. But the screen of the world has hardened our human perception so that the earth and all that's on it appear as material substance. Circumstances, instead of being always helpful, are mostly constricting. Thus do people often find the world not only difficult, but 'hard'.

The ethereal reality is the original divine emanation of the earth.

All inanimate objects and living things are ethereal. With the perception of the survivors no longer worldly, their intelligence will be one with this amazing pristine purity of life on earth.

They will see the earth and every object shimmering in fundamental reality. The images will be semi-transparent and glow from within. Together they will form a beauteous array of soft shimmering light varying constantly in brightness and intensity.

The outlines of the objects will be undefined, like heatwaves. Every object, although separate in its own right, will be connected to everything else, even to the stars, by an even more indefinable ethereality – a supernal, omniscient matrix of intelligence. This, to our worldly perception, is space.

The remarkable thing is that our worldly perception parallels the state of life without the world – with one huge difference. Life without the world is the original cause, and the world is a distorting and misleading effect. (An effect however can never be representative of the cause, and as we proceed I'll draw attention to the world's deceptive parallel perspectives.)

Nevertheless, the manifest purity of the natural earth as we may sometimes see it and love it, is a pure reflection in matter of the pristine reality behind. But any attempt to analyse or name the phenomenon introduces a learned worldly perspective and short-circuits the immediate delight and pleasure.

THEIR KNOWLEDGE OF MEANING

*T*he survivors will apprehend each ethereal image in its *meaning, now* – in a way vaguely similar to how we apprehend objects by recognition.

Recognition however is a worldly perception based on having seen or cognised something in the past. As the survivors will have been freed of the past, and because the ethereal reality is now, there will be no recognition – only immediate knowledge of meaning.

Meaning is the ever-moving value of life perceived without the distorting effect of the world.

In place of being caught up in humanity's futile and problematical search for meaning through personal and collective progress, the survivors will enjoy the constant delight of seeing deeper into the limitless mystery of life.

This is what happens to people on earth in those rare moments when they are truly seeing and loving the beauty of nature – without thinking. On those occasions their intelligence is momentarily one (at-one-ment) with the beauty. But the purity of the moment is quickly obscured by thought which pulls them back into tedious worldly time.

As the wondrous moment of oneness with beauty will be continuous for the survivors, they will be in another time – a new time without meaning to our thinking, worldly selves.

THEIR UNDIVIDED INTELLIGENCE

*T*he key to this amazing life beyond worldliness is that the intelligence of each survivor (which we call individual consciousness or awareness) will be the central point of the vast reality of life on earth. In a similar, though self-conscious way, does everyone in the world unknowingly act and respond as though they were the centre of it all.

The surviving intelligence will be individual in the sense that individual really means un-divided. Being undivided, the intelligence will not be separate from the whole, as our individual consciousness is. Each will be pure perception or pure knowledge – super intelligence without a centre while being a distinct all-connected place in the whole.

Furthermore, each individual survivor will know implicitly that mankind, in its original simplicity, is the intelligence of life on earth.

THEIR DEGREES OF INTELLIGENCE

*A*lthough the survivors will all share the common perception of the ethereal reality, there will be degrees of depth of that perception. Some will be more super-intelligent than others, although all will be far more intelligent than us in the world.

In our world of sluggish, tedious time the intelligence of the population also varies enormously (although we do our best to ignore this). Even so, at birth all share in the same common intelligence of earth without world – unrecognised by the people around them.

Inevitably, the original intelligence is slowly degraded by personalised impressions of the world and attachment to experience thereof – aided by the worldly ignorance of others. In the absence of any common delineator or reality as a guide, ignorance of the world and attachment to the world take over.

The result is that the global population continuously seeks some sort of permanent security and ongoing reassurance – even though both are worldly impossibilities. So they form personal friendships and partnerships with like-minded individuals; and come together through business, political, social and religious affiliations.

Religious affiliations are probably the most dangerous as they can appeal to the destructive extremes of human nature – a fact demonstrated throughout history by religious fanaticism. The key is that all religions refer to self-sacrifice as leading to a better life after death. In extremes of zeal this is taken to mean the sacrifice of the body for a cause, whereas in truth self-sacrifice means the sacrifice of the worldly self responsible for such unholy notions and beliefs.

The frightening thing is that people go to war and kill people *bolstered and self-justified by alliances and allegiances.*

THEIR LOVE OF THE EARTH

*A*lthough no longer attached to the world through alliances and loyalty to causes, some of the survivors will still be attached to the earth. Such attachment – the love of the earth's beauty, the life-forms on it and its continued physical presence – is completely natural and fulfilling, as is experienced by many people in the world. In fact, being in nature is a way most people gain temporary respite from the world.

The crucial difference is that the survivors' loving attachment to the earth won't create problems – such as in people's sense of disturbance at the apparent destruction and exploitation of nature, and their efforts to prevent this. The survivors will be in the reality behind worldly appearances where the purity of nature is untouched and untouchable by the world.

The attachment to the earth will vary in each of these survivors. It will slow the intelligence marginally but without impairing the wondrous fundamental vision. As a result, however, the *meaning* of each object, including the survivor's own presence, will vary very finely and faintly every moment with the incredibly swiftness of now. The slightly different perceptions will add to the scintillating beauty of the whole.

In the world, the parallel of this is that the condition of a person's intelligence determines the impressions and experience they have of people and objects. The difference is that in reality there is only pure meaning and no impressions or experience because impressions and experience are the products of worldly time. So everyone in the world – despite alliances and allegiances – also tends to see things differently; but with the differences frequently leading to misunderstandings and personal confusion.

Another parallel is that in our world, love of the earth and the life on it manifests as a certain sensitivity to natural beauty. This usually expresses itself in some art form, or in an unrequited longing to be creative – both of which invariably involve frustration. But unlike in our world, the survivors' love of the earth will allow the intelligence to function creatively, without restriction, over an amazingly profound and fulfilling range.

Although all the survivors will see the ethereality of the earth as described, those still attached to the earth will have what I can only describe as dual vision. On one hand they will see the shimmering translucent reality, and on the other, everything will have substantive form. In the play of intelligence as meaning, their perception will be of both states at once. A great blessing – which will not be at all disturbing (as it is in the little-understood worldly condition labelled schizophrenia).

For those few no longer attached to the earth there will be only the ethereal reality. As the ethereal reality is the essence behind the formal beauty of the earth, these survivors will have no need of the physical. But, as purified intelligence, they will still be perceived in essence and love by the others.

The less there is of earthly attachment, the less is the need for physical bodies – and therefore of procreation.

Their Love, and Sex

*S*ex as such will not exist for the survivors, since the drive of sex is responsible for most of the unhappiness on earth. Sex is the *unconscious* universal craving to find love. But as love is a *conscious* earthly quality, sex misses the point and leaves a trail of unhappiness, violence and war – all of which can only find expression in the world.

There will be no sex without love. Sex in reality is simply attraction. As love is the fundamental quality of life, attraction will have purpose. Indiscriminate self-gratification and sexual exploitation of others will have vanished with the world.

The division between the genders of male and female also will not exist. The genders exist only in division, and it is our worldly perception that divides them. Man and woman will exist. But the way of perceiving and enjoying each other will be completely different.

Today our perception of the opposite sex is the worldly result of thousands of years of developing sexual imagination. Sexual imagination or fantasy is a strictly personal, and therefore selfish, stimulation. It has reached a compulsive global intensity now evident in every walk of life – from the mainstream movies, the media ads, the fashions, and the sexual liberation propaganda, to the undeniable personal experience of every man and woman.

The sexual imagination – lurid or not so lurid – has corrupted the natural procreative instinct in both genders. The instinct is still there of course but it is now largely driven and manipulated by fantasy and sexual imagery.

The final world calamity will eliminate the need of sexual imagination in the survivors. Each will perceive the other direct as each is. Couples will come together out of pure attraction which is infallible, instead of dubious personal selection and preference.

In other words, the survivors will be male and female bodies with nothing between them but purpose and love.

In the reality – where there is no world – man and woman unite to form the one super intelligence of life on earth.

THEIR ABSENCE OF HOPE OR BELIEF

*T*he population of the survivors will be controlled by life with the same precision as the regularity of the seasons and all that is natural. There will be no personal wanting or wishing to interfere with the rhythm of life. Death will no longer exist because the presence and oneness with never-ending life will have removed all fear and made death irrelevant.

The survivors will love all things, as they will see the reality in all things through the reality of their own perception. They will not have personal likes and dislikes; and, being one with endless life, no need of hope or belief.

Life, the great intelligence of the earth, will guide them moment to moment without any sense, or need, of personal involvement. They will simply do as they do in a state of intense love and delight – and what they do will be right.

Nothing will be fixed or static. Every moment will be an extremely fine overall descent into a greater purity – the power and knowledge of unlimited life. The constant inner pull will originate in the source of life itself which will never be known or need to be known by any surviving intelligence. The wondrous reality of participation will be enough.

In contrast, the compulsion of the world is to try to know, and then to know more when all that can be known is the world. This gives rise to material science, speculation and invention without regard for the *source* of it all.

As a result, we in the world are compelled to be seemingly dragged along by the force of progress, not realising that we're not being pulled at all, but are being pushed by our own thirst to know more – more burdensome information mistakenly called knowledge.

Nevertheless, there is an implacable and irresistible pull familiar to everyone in the world but not discerned as the cause of their periodic discontent, dissatisfaction and unhappiness. The pull of Source does not allow anybody to remain content, satisfied or at rest for long. All are kept moving and changing as the Source, acting through the tedious time of living and the swiftness of death, *compassionately* draws intelligent life back towards reality.

Their Unique Originality

The uninhibited creativity of the survivors will lie in the simple *unique* quality each one of us is beneath the personal facade of learning, studying and struggling to achieve or be recognised. If everyone was their unique originality, and no longer their own worldly person, there would be no necessity for competing or struggling.

Such is life when the world has been eradicated from the individual.

'Unique' means being without a like or equal. It's not a form of life. It *is* life. When everyone is unique there's only continuous harmonious acknowledgement – one to the other and of the whole.

We who are living now can't comprehend the whole because we perceive through the fragmented world of what each of us has learned and experienced. The result is countless opinions, advice and points of view – no single, meaningful focus.

The survivors of the end of the world, however, will have a common simple and straightforward viewpoint and a certainty of knowledge which we can never have.

They will be seeing and appreciating the unique quality of each other, not as personal differences as we do, but as utterly inseparable parts of the amazing ethereal *whole* of life.

The whole of life, which escapes our narrowed perception, will be the immediate knowledge informing the survivors. They will know without doubt that life is sustaining the earth, themselves and everything every moment.

And their dedication to serving the purity of life within and without will be absolute.

By virtue of the unique quality of each (virtue means worthiness), the survivors will initiate a new way of life on earth beyond all imagining. That will be the vehicle for their unlimited creativity and love.

THE WORK OF BARRY LONG

The audio tape on which this book is based – 'The End of the World' – is still available and can be ordered from The Barry Long Foundation International through the contact addresses at back. The tape was originally part of a series called 'The Myth of Life'. The other tapes in this series are now in the Barry Long Audio collection: 'Start Meditating Now', 'A Journey in Consciousness', 'Seeing Through Death', 'Making Love' and 'How To Live Joyously' all of which can be ordered either from the Foundation or through bookstores.

A large number of audio and video recordings of Barry Long's teaching meetings are supplied by The Foundation directly by mailorder and a full catalogue can be supplied on request. The current updated catalogue of all Barry Long's books and tapes may be viewed online at www.barrylong.org together with selected teaching statements, articles and biographical information.

Barry Long lives in northern New South Wales, Australia. He holds afternoon meetings on the Gold Coast of Queensland at which he often speaks on topical issues. These are recorded and 'Gold Coast Talks Tapes' are released shortly after each meeting. More intensive sessions of three to fourteen days are held several times a year which attract audiences of several hundred people from all over the world. Videos of his meetings are shown in many countries.

Barry Long is 75 years old (at the time of writing) and his health no longer permits him to travel or teach far from home. Nevertheless the impact of his teaching is seen world-wide. His best-selling books circulate in tens of thousands and his work is published in ten languages.

OTHER BOOKS BY BARRY LONG

ONLY FEAR DIES – A book of liberation

A radical book on how to achieve real freedom.

This is a book of essays on the causes and effects of unhappiness and the spiritual process of 'dying for life'. It shows us what we can do to release ourselves from the tensions of living, and challenges us to give up our 'right to be unhappy'. The perspective then shifts to the world scene – helping us to disengage from the mass delusions of the human condition. Barry Long also has prophetic things to say about the way the world is going.

'*A wake up call.*' MAGICAL BLEND

THE WAY IN – A book of self-discovery

Essential statements of love, truth, God, stillness, now . . .

The ways of truth, meditation, prayer and love. How to reach the ultimate truth for ourselves. How to avoid the pitfalls and delusions of the spiritual path. And finally the end of every spiritual search. This is a survey of the entire process of spiritual realisation - placing the whole responsibility on the individual, with no intermediary belief systems. This is the most complete statement in one volume of Barry Long's teaching. A great source of inspiration and self-discovery.

This book also contains a revised version of the original text of 'The End of the World'.

'This simple to read, but spiritually advanced book offers immense insight into the truth within us.' GOLDEN AGE

THE ORIGINS OF MAN AND THE UNIVERSE
The myth that came to life

The cosmos, consciousness and your part in the whole scheme.

This work of immense vision tells the whole story of how we and the earth got here – from the Big Bang to the coming

End of Time. Relates our inner life to the outer world in ways that draw us deeper into a solution for the ultimate question, the one that every human being has asked down all the ages: What is beyond the heavens? What's behind it all? What on earth are we doing here?

One of the chapters deals insightfully and prophetically with civilisation, violence, war and terrorism.

'A profound and spellbinding book by one of the world's greatest masters. This book is destined to become a classic.' THE PLANET

KNOWING YOURSELF – The true in the false

A remarkable statement of spiritual self-discovery.

This book is a collection of observations about life, truth, love and death made while the author was undergoing an intense process of self-realisation. These fresh, clear, challenging insights are a map for us as we follow our own spiritual journey into self-knowledge. As you read you discover the difference between love and emotion, joy and sentiment, your will and your desire, and you see what lies behind all human motivation.

'A book to be highly recommended.' YOGA TODAY

MEDITATION A FOUNDATION COURSE – A book of ten lessons

Practical exercises to do in everyday life.

A no-nonsense practical course which is very clear and easy to follow. Step by step you learn to still your busy mind and learn how to deal with worry. The concise lessons give practical exercises you can use at home and at work. Free of esoteric or religious overtones. This is practical, effective meditation now and puts you on the road to a more harmonious, fulfilling life.

'One of the most practical guides to meditation on the market.'
NEW AGE GUARDIAN

STILLNESS IS THE WAY – An intensive meditation course

Advanced meditation and spiritual practice.

This book is an inspiring guide to self-knowledge, in the form of an intensive three day course. To read it is to participate in the course and do, be and feel the reality it communicates. It takes us through the restlessness and confusion often encountered in spiritual practice and goes beyond the formal devices of sitting meditation. It introduces us to a state of consciousness in which we may live more freely and naturally – where the words such as truth, love and grace are no longer abstractions but living reality.

'It is thrilling to discover a reliable guide on this path of meditation. Barry Long is a remarkable teacher whose words have the certainty of a deeply realised being.' MEDITATION MAGAZINE

MAKING LOVE – Sexual love the divine way

Sexual love addressed honestly and originally.

This book offers a life-changing encounter with real love; a way to keep love constantly fresh and alive through honest, pure and conscious lovemaking. A unique and radical tantric teaching that transforms your relationships and brings the dream of true love closer to reality. Gives lovemaking its due place in the spiritual life. Essential reading for anyone who is serious in the search for real love.

A landmark bestseller, this book has transformed the love-life of thousands worldwide.

Also available on audio tape.

'The most profound insights on love and sexuality that you are ever likely to encounter.' NEW AGE GUARDIAN

WISDOM AND WHERE TO FIND IT - A book of truth

Describes a beautiful and radically different way to live.

In the early phases of self-discovery we question life's purpose and our relationship to wider society. This book tackles some of the vital questions: What is 'good'? What is truth? Why does mankind suffer? Do we really have control over our lives? Why am I alive? It teaches self-observation in a way relevant to ordinary life.

'An ideal introduction to Barry Long which whets the appetite for more.' SCIENCE OF THOUGHT REVIEW

RAISING CHILDREN IN LOVE, JUSTICE AND TRUTH

Practical parenting advice with a spiritual dimension.

This is a compendium of advice given by Barry Long to parents who have asked him for help in handling family relationships. It is largely a book of dialogues and conversations, grounding the spiritual dimension in actual case histories. The very many topics cover familiar domestic situations as well as more difficult problems, such as how to help children cope with grief and how to help teenagers come to terms with their sexual awakening.

'Parents looking for a spiritual guide to raising their children need look no further than Barry Long's extraordinary book. You are in for an invigorating journey, face-to-face with one of the world's most direct, simple spiritual masters who also happens to know about paying the bills every month!' NATURAL PARENT

TO WOMAN IN LOVE – A book of letters

Touching the heart of the matter for every woman.

A book of letters about love, its pain and transcending beauty, written by women of all ages from many countries to a man who offers the purity of a divine love beyond personal considerations. Barry Long's replies are intimate, challenging, compassionate letters to Woman, his beloved.

'A work of honesty and love that will speak to many.' ADYAR BOOKNEWS

TO MAN IN TRUTH – Enlightening letters

Straight, plain speaking advice for men.

This book is a selection of letters to Barry Long from men endeavouring to live the spiritual life. The letters and replies are testimony to the sometimes agonising inner conflict that men experience between the inner drive towards truth and the pressures of living and working in the world. The time comes for all of them when they must discover for them-selves what really impels them, what it is that they really love. Always revealing, Barry Long's answers are incisive, compassionate, practical and profound.

'Long speaks about how love can be used to strengthen each man's connection with the great mystery.' CONSCIOUS LIVING

BARRY LONG AUDIO BOOKS

START MEDITATING NOW

A JOURNEY IN CONSCIOUSNESS

SEEING THROUGH DEATH

MAKING LOVE

HOW TO LIVE JOYOUSLY

Above books & audio available from the Foundation or bookshops.

CONTACT DETAILS

For a complete catalogue of Barry Long's current books, tapes, videos and teaching program contact:

THE BARRY LONG FOUNDATION INTERNATIONAL
A non-profit charitable organisation

AUSTRALIA ~ Box 5277, Gold Coast MC, Queensland 4217

ENGLAND ~ BCM Box 876, London, WC1N 3XX

USA ~ Suite 251, 6230 Wilshire Boulevard,
          Los Angeles, CA 90048. *Or call* 1 800 4971081

EMAIL ~ info@barrylong.org

Current details of Barry Long's work along with statements, articles and biographical information can be found online at:

WEBSITE: ~ www.barrylong.org